S0-BOC-234

Visual Manna's Drawing, Painting and Sculpting Horses

by

Rich and Sharon Jeffus

We would like to dedicate this book to two wonderful aunts who are both artists. These ladies have been an inspiration in the field of art. We thank God for them and their precious influence. Thanks so much Helen Goodwin and Anne Smith!

Copyright 2001

Deuteronomy 20:1 When thou goest out to battle against thine enemies, and seest horses, and chariots, and a people more than thou, be not afraid of them; for the Lord thy God is with thee, which brought thee out of the land of Egypt.

ISDN 0-9715970-0-6

Table of Contents

Introduction

An inscription written in the Horse Park of Kentucky reads, "History was written on the back of the horse." This sounds like a pretty bold statement until you study the real impact the horse has had on civilization.

An easy way is to look at the cultures that did not naturally possess the magnificent horse and compare them with cultures that did. The Americas did not have the horse. Most early Americans remained scattered and underdeveloped. They were a population of hunter gatherers. Individual tribes had little or no interaction with other tribes. The only great cultures of the Americas were the Incas, Mayans, and Aztecs. Even though these developed great societies, they were never able to spread their knowledge very far.

Other examples of this inability to get past the small tribal units can be seen in other horseless parts of the world such as Australia and the Sahara part of Africa..

The earliest evidence of horse domestication has been found in the eastern Ukraine, northern Caucasus, central Russia and Kazakhstan. They were probably first hunted for meat. When mankind learned to keep them as herd animals, they were probably still used for meat but also for milk (as nomads in central Asia still do today).

Horses were taught to drag possessions and to pull carts. Horses were probably not ridden at first. For one thing, the early horses were a lot smaller than they are today. This isn't because they were evolving from some rock hydrix, but were just small horses. They were about the size of a large pony. Mankind probably learned early on how to breed the biggest mares with the biggest stallions to make a bigger horse. There is good evidence that people were riding horses by the end of the first millennium. The first account of riding a horse in the Bible is Gen. 49:17 "Dan shall be a serpent by the way, an adder in the path, that bite the horse heels, so that his rider shall fall backward." There is even an older book in the Bible. It is perhaps the oldest book in the world. It is the book of Job. In it, we find these interesting verses about riding horses and battles.

Job 39:18 What time she lifteth up herself (talking about an ostrich) on high, she scorneth the horse and his rider.
19* Hast thou given the horse strength? Hast thou clothed his neck with thunder?
20* Canst thou make him afraid as a grasshopper? The glory of his nostrils is terrible.
21* He paweth in the valley, and rejoiceth in his strength: he goeth on to meet the armed men.
22* He mocketh at fear, and is not affrighted; neither turneth he back from the sword.
23* The quiver rattleth against him, the glittering spear and the shield.
24* He swalloweth the ground with fierceness and rage: neither believeth he that it is the sound of the trumpet.
25* He saith among the trumpets, Ha, ha; and he smelleth the battle afar off, the thunder of the captains, and the shouting.

These early references to battle and the horse indicate what really happened when mankind was able to move farther, expand hunting ranges, and encounter others more easily. They explored the ends of the earth, and then fought over them.

The Hittites invented the war chariot. With this new invention they conquered Mesopotamia and Egypt. This new terrible war machine was farther advanced than a fighter aircraft is to a rifleman.

The horse became known as a symbol of power and privilege. The number of your horses became a measure of your wealth. 1 Kings 4:26, " And Solomon had forty thousand stalls of horses for his chariots, and twelve thousand horsemen."

The Persians developed a means of communicating with the far reaches of their empire using the horse. Their system was much like the Pony Express system set up in the American west in the 19th century. It is said of these couriers by Herodotus, "neither snow, rain, heat, nor darkness stays from the swift completion of their appointed rounds." These words were adopted by the U.S. Post Office as its motto.

Many say that the use of horses for work was slow in coming. This is partly because they were small and expensive to keep. This made them no match for the oxen which could pull plows and carts. Horses became heavier. The heavy draft horse was developed by the Germanic tribes of the north. These large breeds became very useful when the horse collar, (invented in China), arrived in Europe. There had been many different methods of attaching horses to chariots; but nothing that harnessed the power from the horses shoulder like the horse collar. Using this new invention and the larger draft horses, the farmers could plow larger fields and move more produce to market faster.

Probably the next great invention that changed the horse's usefulness was the invention of the stirrup. The stirrup came to the west around the 8th century. This was a revolution as big as the chariot. This invention allowed heavily armored men to mount a horse. It also allowed them to wield battle axes, thrust lances, and hack with swords without falling off. These mounted warriors with their armored horses became the new weapon of choice. One of these fully armored and outfitted war horses had to carry as much as 400 pounds. These knights became so vital to warfare that a landlord's position was measured in how many knights he could provide to the king. This was in exchange for protection. This was the beginning of the feudal system.

The feudal system provided for some stability. With this the horse was put to work pulling plows, stagecoaches, and walking on treadmills to provide the power for industry. Even the first trains were horse-drawn on their steel tracks.

For thousands of years, until the invention of the internal combustion engine, horses and horse-drawn vehicles were the only effective means to cover large distances, plow the soil, transport merchandise, and wage war. For just one species, the influence of the horse has been immeasurably profound. Perhaps it was said best in an Arabian Proverb which says, "The horse is God's gift to man."

4

Using Supplies

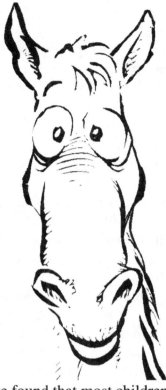

Here are some helpful hints on using art supplies for children. I hope you will enjoy this information, and add it to your data base. I am a great believer in using recycled supplies and saving money on paper, mat board, etc. so you can spend more money on oil pastels, paints, and chalks so children can experience many different media as they do their art. In my Visual Manna I Complete Art Curriculum, there are many suggestions for using materials and supplies. Add this to your information!

Markers, Pencils and Colored Pencils

I have found that most children in the second grade and up benefit with an optional eraser and pencil to begin a project For younger children, I usually put oil pastels and markers on the table for coloring projects. I dispense with pencils. Sharpening pencils for little ones can become a bigger thrill then the art project itself! Little ones always benefit, I believe, from having choices and options where media is concerned. The quality of markers and colored pencils for younger children is not important. However, as they get older and more advanced in their art, I recommend Pentel markers and Berol or Prismacolor pencils. I believe an Ebony drawing pencil is the best for older student use. Art projects do benefit with quality materials. Mixed media projects are always a good idea for children. Giving them a variety of materials within the framework of a particular project allows for creativity.

The circle on the left shows the primary colors of the color wheel. The circle on the right shows the secondary colors. Have students color in the rest of both color wheels.

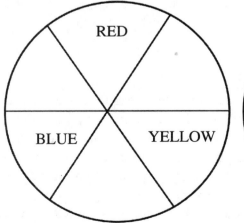

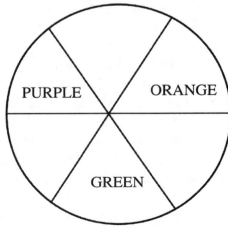

Using Oil Pastels

Oil pastels are a wonderful medium for children. They love the bright colors. Encourage children to color darkly. You want the picture to look opaque, so you cannot see the white paper through the color. Oil pastels really should look like paint when the composition is finished. Oil pastels are great to teach the mixing and blending of color. In the higher quality variety of oil pastels, you can even take turpentine on the end of the brush and blend. These are good to use with younger children because they are not messy. We like the Studio Basic oil pastels for students: 24 color variety.

Using Tempera Paints

This is a delightful medium for children, and a special treat for some. Younger children experience great success using the plastic container daubers. Children paint with the tip of the bottle. There is little mess, as you don't need to worry about spills. You don't need to worry about little ones putting their red brush into the yellow color. I personally don't like using cake tempera with children. If you are using mixed tempera paints in an open container, add a little liquid detergent to the bottle. This does not affect the color, but makes clean up a little easier. I believe, if you are mixing dry paint, baby food jars work best for storing paint. Baby food jars are also good to set on the tables with clean water to clean brushes. We have found some flat containers that can sit on the tables and are practically impossible to tip over. They were found by accident at a local restaurant supply store. The latest research shows that even young children can use a variety of brush sizes. Previously, younger children were only given large brushes, but now research indicates they can do better if given a variety of brush sizes to choose from. Some will choose larger brushes, others will choose smaller brushes.

Using Water Color Paint

I believe it is best to use Prang watercolors for younger children, or colors of a higher quality. Some of the cheaper watercolors do not work well and fade over time. You need to stress with children when you do projects using watercolor, to work light. Use light colors because you can always get darker, but you cannot get lighter. The more water you use in proportion to the paint, the lighter your color will be. You can use salt, or a blow hair dryer for effect in your picture. You can take a toothbrush and splatter paint on your picture. You can do a number of other creative things. For more instructions, see <u>Visual Manna I and II Complete Curriculums.</u> There you can find out about wet and dry brush techniques, etc.

Using Chalk Pastels

Many times chalk pastels are taught before learning oil or acrylic painting, because of the ability to mix this medium. Colored paper is often used to enhance the finished product. You need to tell children to use lots of chalk to achieve an opaque look. Blend and mix colors as much as possible. Layering colors also works well. White and black charcoal pencils work well to detail your finished picture. Starting with a sunset is a good idea, because you can really learn to blend colors well. You can purchase pastel paper at your local craft store, or just use colored construction paper. Pastel paper or a very fine sand paper helps with achieving an opaque look. Remember to use a can of aerosol hair spray to cover the finished work. This way there will be no messy smearing of the finished work of art.

Horses are a very important part of history. They have played prominent parts in the history of many countries and especially the American west. If you love horses and want to learn how to draw, sculpt and paint horses, you will love this book! We are going to look at the horse in art history, and particularly in the history of the American west. There are many project ideas to create your own portfolio of horse art.

Horse Facts

Very young horses are called *foals*. Adult full grown females are called *mares*. Adult males are called *stallions*.

Look back on our struggle for freedom,
 Trace our present day's strength to its source;
And you'll find that man's pathway to glory
 Is strewn with the bones of a horse.
Anonymous

Equine: A horse, or having to do with horses

Equestrian: Someone who rides or interacts with horses

Equitation: The art and practice of riding a horse

Common name: Horse

Scientific name: Equus caballus

Habitat: open fields, grasslands

Foods: grasses and grains

Predators: man and large meat-eaters

Drawing the Horse

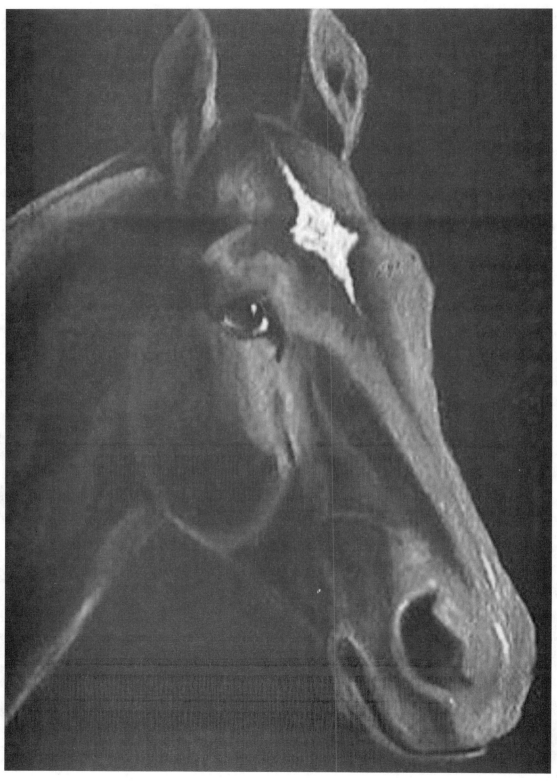

Study the bone and muscle structure of the horse carefully.
Horses have 175 bones in their body.

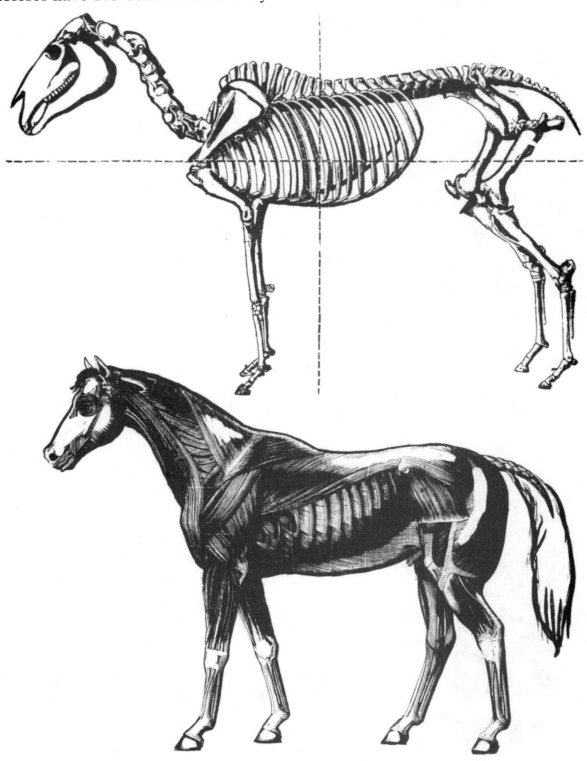

Practice drawing the skeleton in pencil first. Many master artists such as Leonardo da Vinci and Michelangelo studied anatomy carefully.

Horse Drawing Ages 4 Through 8

This is a process drawing of a horse for little ones ages four through eight. Basic shapes can be remembered when drawing this horse.

Pinto pony

It is not enough for a man to know how to ride; he must know how to fall.
Mexican Proverb

Just like when you fall off a horse, you get back on and ride again; when you draw your first horse, you must not be discouraged, but get your pencil and draw again. The more you practice, the better horse artist you will be!

10

Shading a cylinder or a sphere.

The quickest way to make something look three dimensional is to apply, shading, shadow and texture.

The purpose of shading is to make the object dark on one side and light on the other, with the easiest gradient as possible.

LIGHT

Draw a cylinder.

Pick the direction the light
is coming from.

fig.1

shade. #3 is just straight lines, the more lines the darker. #4 is contour lines. These lines follow the shape. The lines are made longest first, and then shorter and shorter lines are added between each line. #5 is shading made by a pile of pencil lead (graphite) placed on the paper and spread out with a smudge stick or forefinger.

LIGHT

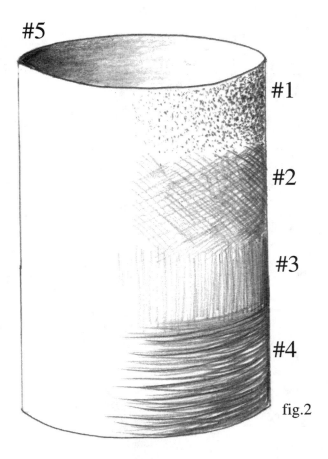

fig.2

Shade the cylinder. Try several techniques to determine which one you like best. Some techniques may work better for you on one kind of picture than another, so get familiar with all of them.

In fig.2, I used several techniques on the same cylinder. #1 is stippling; the use of dots or points; the more dots, the darker the shading. #2 is cross hatching, the more cross hatch the darker the

A large part of being an artist is being observant. Take your drawings and really look at them. Turn them upside down and look carefully. Turn them over on the back and look through the paper, by holding it up to a light. What do you see? Are all the vertical lines really vertical. Get a straight edge and lay it along a supposed straight line, is it straight? Next time as you begin drawing, remember what you observed and make corrections before you darken your lines.

This sphere, fig.1, was shaded with a combination of techniques. Draw several basic shapes and shade them in using various techniques. Try doing cones, cylinders, rods and spheres.

fig.1

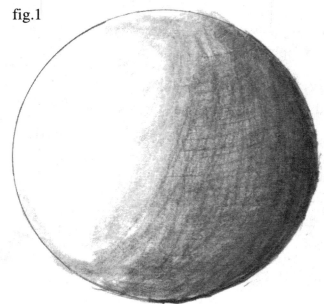

This is an example of a sphere shaded with a single light source.

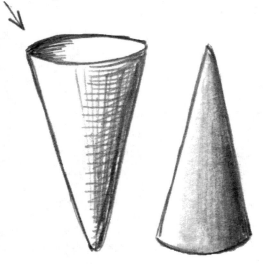

Cones

So far we have been doing objects with curved surfaces.

Notice this example of incorrect shading below. The cube's sides look rounded. This is because the use of a gradient makes the flat sides curve. I would not say, "Never shade like this." Someday you may want a metallic look. Which is what the cube below looks like. But in general, to make a cube look "right", keep each side flat by the use of uniform shading as explained earlier.

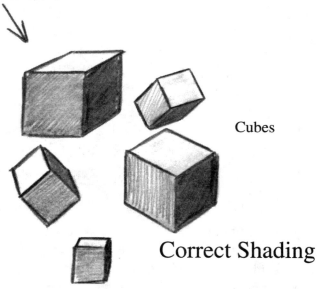

Cubes

Correct Shading

When you shade things with flat sides such as cubes, you shade each side the same tone, like the ones above. This is because the side is not curved. Each side should have a slightly different shade, depending on the light source.

Incorrect Shading

As part of this lesson find some real objects that represent basic shapes. Cylinder shapes for example are hair spray cans, flashlight batteries, soup cans, paper towel rolls, bananas, carrots or telescopes. Sphere shapes are, marbles, balls, green peas, frog eggs, oranges or apples. Get several examples and draw them from different angles. Be careful to draw what you see, not what you think you see. A good artist is a good observer.

On the previous two pages you have learned about shading. In all your pictures, you will need to shade your horses correctly. Here is another wonderful way to draw a horse.

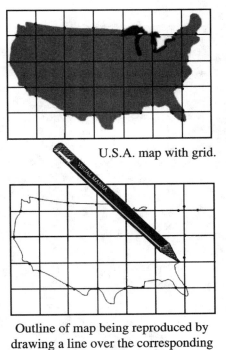

U.S.A. map with grid.

Outline of map being reproduced by drawing a line over the corresponding points of the grid.

How to Use a Grid

In this book there are opportunities to do drawings using the grid. This is an optional way to copy a master work of art. Many artists in the past and artists today use a grid in their work. Copying great works of art is one way to learn technique and grow as an artist.

Following are directions for using a grid. There are two ways to use a grid. One way is to do the entire outline first, and then go back and complete the inside. The other way is to do one single square at a time, completing each one before going on to the next. Whichever way you use, try to remember to draw what you see, and not what you think you see. Doing a grid can help you become a better artist by letting you see the relationship between each separate part of a whole drawing. Remember that using a grid is only one way of several in which an artist uses to copy a picture. For a complete lesson on the grid go to <visualmanna.com>.

Implied Grid

There is an alternate method to a formal grid. It is called an implied grid. What you do is draw one piece of the picture, and use that piece to measure the rest of the picture. Below is a picture of a horse. I am going to draw it using the ear as a measurement.

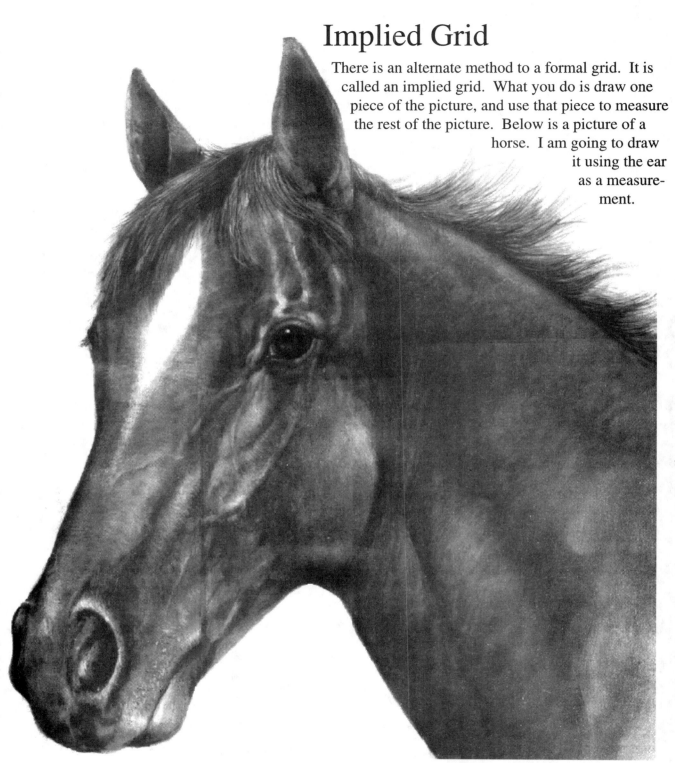

All artists do the same thing. They start by doing an outline drawing. Sometimes they use a formal grid, sometimes an implied grid, and sometimes they just draw it. Most artists, however, use some form of implied grid. Most do this without thinking, but they are always looking at how one part of the picture lines up with another. Most artists will look at the picture as a whole. They do not focus, as most children do, on the details. They look at the general layout of the whole picture first, and then move on to the details. The method on the following pages will help you see the whole picture.

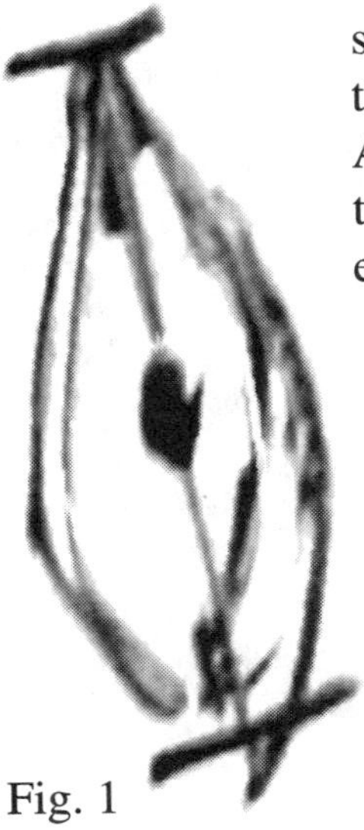

Fig. 1 is a sketch of the horse's ear. Notice the center line. The angle of that line should be the same as the center line drawn on the picture of the horse in Fig. 2. Also in Fig. 3 you can see the top, bottom, and middle of the ear is marked.

Fig. 2

The top and bottom marks give the length that will determine the finished size of the picture. The middle mark will give you an anchor point for much of this picture. It is important to note that you don't have to draw on the

Fig. 1

original picture. It is only drawn on here for an example. It is also important to note that this picture of a horse is unique. This method will work on any picture, but the proportions and relationship between parts of each picture is unique to that picture. In Fig. 3, you can see lines drawn from the center of the ear down the back of the neck, across the forehead and straight down to a place at the highest part of the front of the neck. These lines are reproduced with their angles on a blank sheet of paper,

Fig. 3

shown here in Fig. 4. You can see the ear is drawn in. It will be used to determine the length of the lines. The lines are construction lines. They are not the horse's neck. They only represent the direc-

Fig. 4

tion the neck is running. Remember this is a general layout of a horse. If you are doing this picture right, it will not look like a horse until the final stages. The next page will show you how the size of the ear will determine the size of your finished drawing.

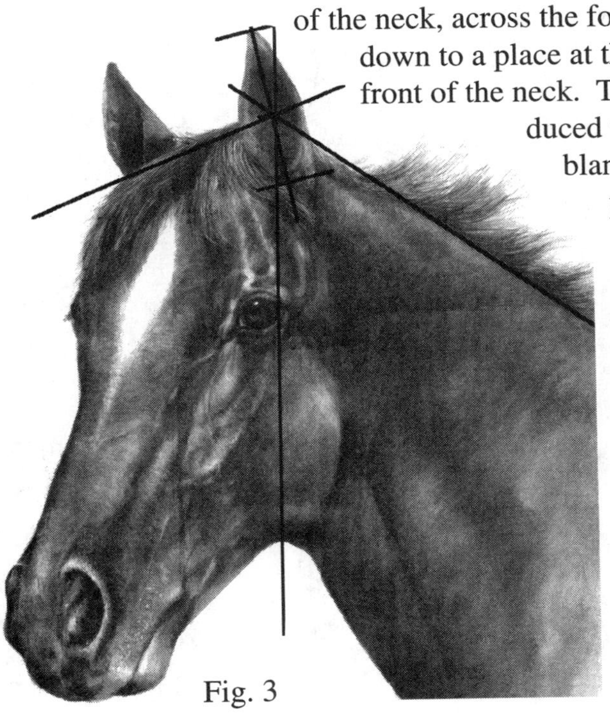

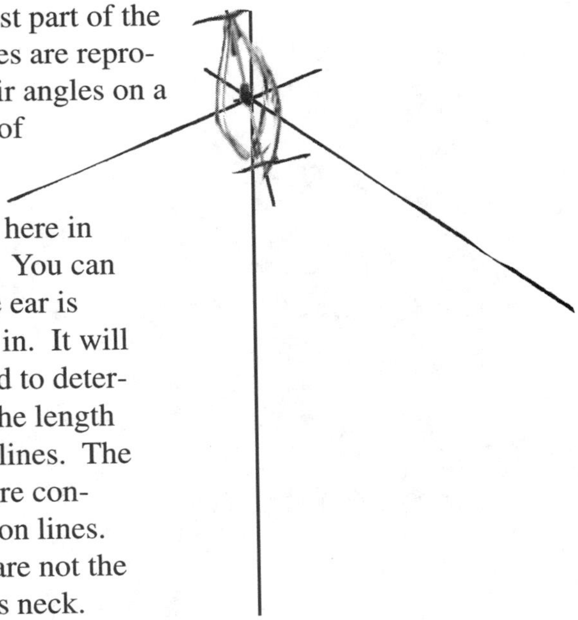

On your drawing, if you make the ear 2 inches long, the finished drawing will be about 8 inches tall. If you draw it 2 feet long, you will need a sheet of paper at least 8 feet tall!

It is easy to see in Fig.5 that it takes 3 and 1/4 ears lengths to go from the top of the horse's ear to the highest part of its neck.

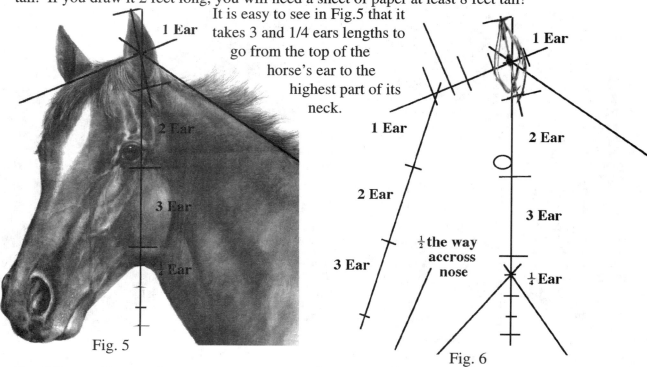

Fig. 5

Fig. 6

Fig. 6 shows the rest of the layout of the horse. Note the placement of the second ear. It is critical to get it in the right place. Artists not only look at what they are drawing, but at what is not drawn.. There is something called positive and negative space. Many people just view this as light and dark. There is another kind. That is easily shown by the space between the horse's ears. The ear is the posi-

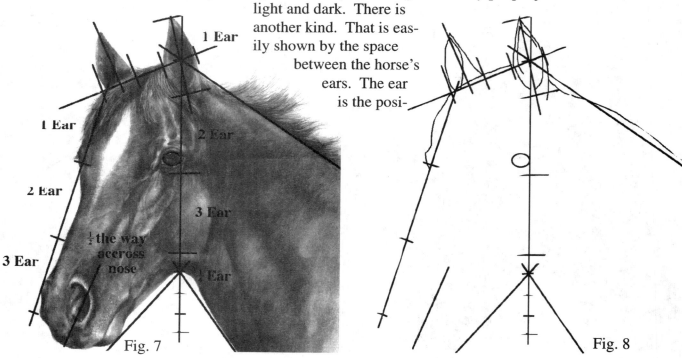

Fig. 7

Fig. 8

tive and the space is the negative. You could see if you drew a perfect ear, but placed it too far or too close from the other ear; the horse would look funny. On this horse, the placement is about the same distance as the first ear's width. With the ear placed correctly, you can place the line down the front of the horse's head. You can see in Fig. 8 that this line is about 3 ears long.

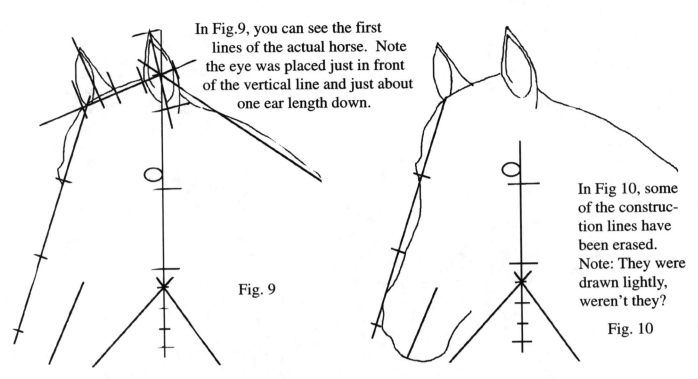

In Fig.9, you can see the first lines of the actual horse. Note the eye was placed just in front of the vertical line and just about one ear length down.

Fig. 9

In Fig 10, some of the construction lines have been erased. Note: They were drawn lightly, weren't they?

Fig. 10

Fig. 11 shows the detail of how the end of the horse's nose is drawn. The nostril is drawn on the center line that is halfway from the chin to the front side of the nose.

More construction lines are erased. Now it is starting to look like a horse! Fig. 12 is the completed outline drawing. It looks pretty good. Many young artists would stop right here. Good enough! But it can be better!

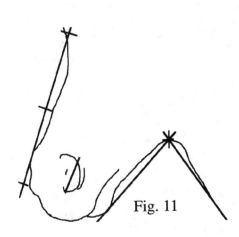

Fig. 11

Fig.12

Every time you complete an outline drawing, you should think: **shading - shadows - textures.** Look at the original picture on page 16. Squint your eyes at it. Look for darkness. Look back at your outline drawing. What is missing? Shading, shadows and textures! As you squint your eyes, it can help you see the dark areas better. Look on the next page for the completed drawing.

This picture was done in pen and ink. Pen and ink is easy. First, do a pencil sketch. The ink is done over the pencil. What makes it so easy is you only go over the lines you want to keep. No matter how many mistakes there were in your original pencil sketch, only the correct lines do you put ink on. When you are all done, just erase any pencil lines left. A gum eraser works best.

These lines represent the center lines of the horse.

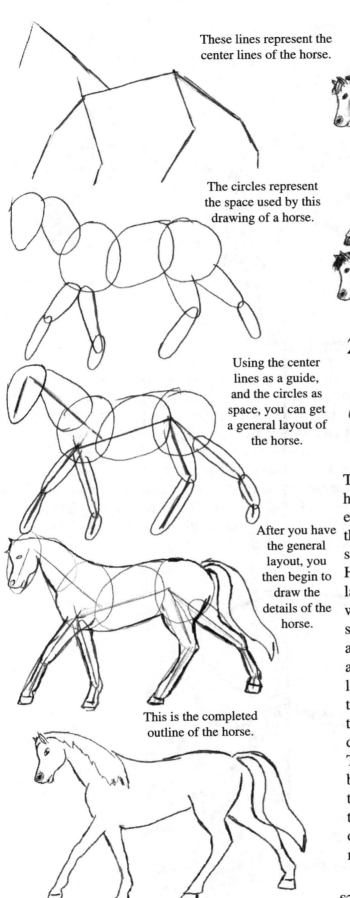

The circles represent the space used by this drawing of a horse.

Using the center lines as a guide, and the circles as space, you can get a general layout of the horse.

After you have the general layout, you then begin to draw the details of the horse.

This is the completed outline of the horse.

1

Which of these two shaded horses looks better?

2

Notice the horse's legs. How does a horse move its legs? Answer at the bottom of the page.

The artist's method of using lines and circles has several advantages. Have you ever started a picture and when you were half way through, you realized that you should have started at a different place on your page? Have you ever wanted to draw a magnificent large horse that filled the whole page, but when you were finished, it was a little scrawny looking horse shape in the middle of a whole page? Well, the use of center lines and circles will help you get your picture looking more like you intended. It is easier to figure out how you want the legs, where the head is looking, and what the horse is doing by first starting out with a stick horse. The circles are useful to give the horse its bulk. As you draw the circles you can make the horse as wide as you want. All of these techniques help you look at the general layout of the horse before going on to the details that make a horse.

Answer: 2 is correct because a horse moves opposite legs at the same time.

When getting the basic shape of a horse, you can begin with circles and ovals shown here. Do basic shapes **lightly** in pencil first and then go over them and detail and refine your drawing. The basic shapes are construction lines. They do not represent the horse, only the space the completed picture will occupy. When we start with the basic shapes, it helps us fit the picture to the piece of paper. Have you ever gotten a good start on a picture only to find out too late that you didn't have enough room on the page to complete it? Using basic shapes will help prevent that from happening. Did you ever pick a picture that was a great close up picture that filled the whole page, but when you were done drawing it your picture was small, off center, and looking rather unimpressive? Using basic shapes will help with that too!

light

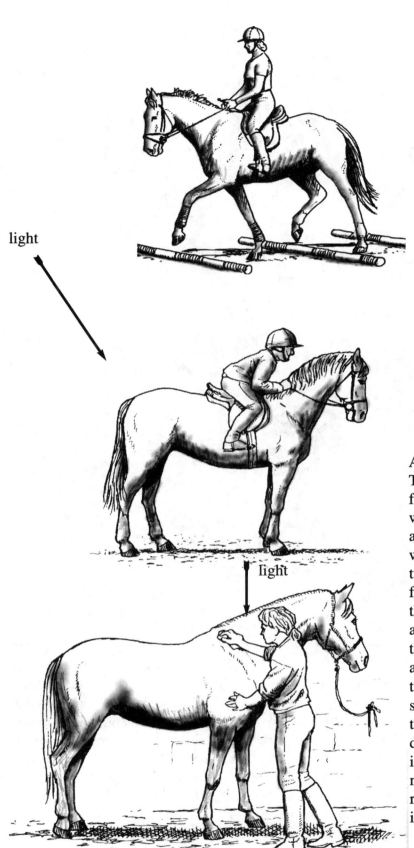

light

light

Observe carefully where the light is coming from. Notice the shading on the stomach of the horse in each instance. In order for your horse drawing to look real, you need to shade it. This will make the body look rounded.

Artists always do one thing. They take real things like flowers, people or horses, which have three dimensions, and turn them into pictures which are flat. To make a picture look more realistic, artists first draw the outline, then they shade it in to provide the appearance of depth. Then they shadow to add realism, and then they give their picture textures. Texture is how something feels. Implied texture is when an artist makes a drawing or painting look like it has texture. You need to make the mane look like it is real hair, and the coat look like it is real hair.

23

This horse is done in a style called stippling. It is comprised of little dots, or points. It is a method of shading that some artists truly love. The advantage of stippling is that it is harder to make mistakes. You are only making one dot at a time. Any dot out of place is only a dot. We all make mistakes. In stippling, the mistakes tend to be small. Most mistakes are made when we get going too fast, becoming impatient or we get bored with what we are doing.

Pointillism-the method of painting using small dots or dabs of color by certain French impressionists.

Stippling is a style that requires great patience. Can you do a horse in this style? Start by lightly, (very lightly), drawing an outline of the horse. Use either a fine point felt-tipped pen or a pen with a tube point. (the tube point pens are the ones that use liquid ink in their barrels). Start making dots where you want the picture dark. Do the shadows and shading first. You don't have to completely finish any area. As you add shading, move around on your picture. You can come back over the same area many times. If you start with the darkest areas and then go on to the next darkest areas, and then back over the same area; the darkest areas become darker as you add to and tie into the next light area. Remember, if you start making too many mistakes, stop! Put down the picture. When you feel rested, pick it back up and start where you left off.

On the left is a picture by Richard Jeffus from a picture by Fredric Remington. The original picture was called, "In From the Night Herd." This Cowboy was the central figure of that picture. The picture first appeared in *Harper's Weekly*, October 9, 1886. Photocopy this page. Below is a lightly drawn outline picture of the picture on the left. Using a fine point pen start filling in the outline. Using stippling, start with the darkest areas and work toward the light.

Diagonal lines show movement! Notice the diagonal lines in the pictures below. Contrast them to the vertical and horizontal lines in the still pictures.

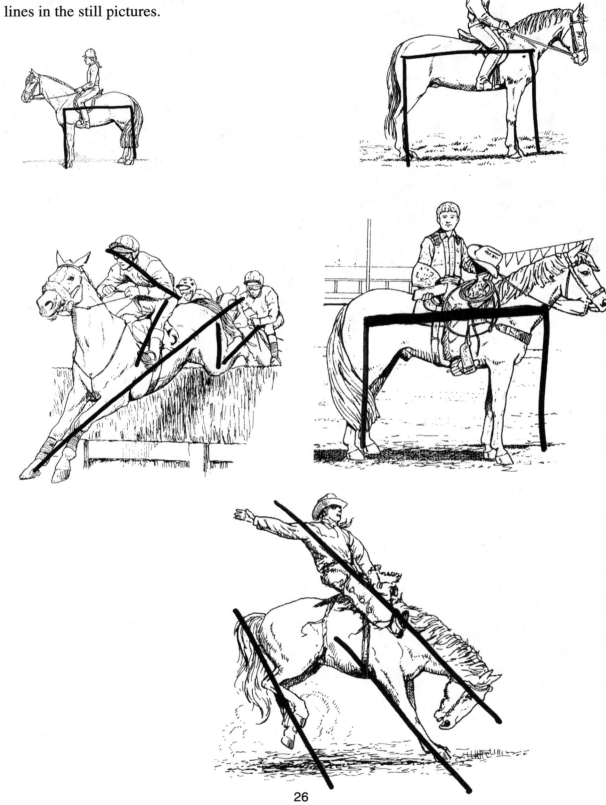

Here are some tips on drawing the horse by one of our favorite horse artists, Martha Cunningham.

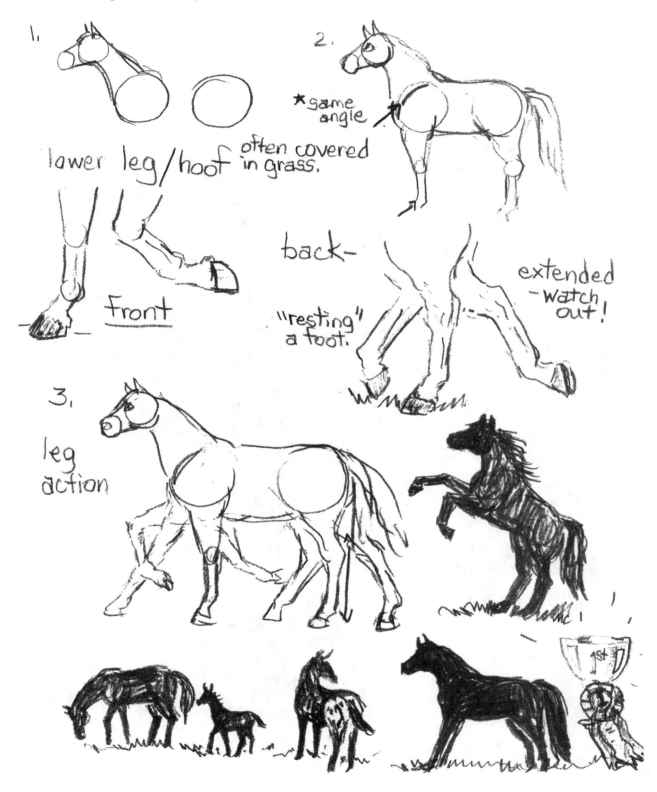

1.

lower leg/hoof often covered in grass.

2.

★ same angle

Front

back-

"resting" a foot.

extended - watch out!

3.

leg action

Here are some tips on drawing a horse head by Martha Cunningham.

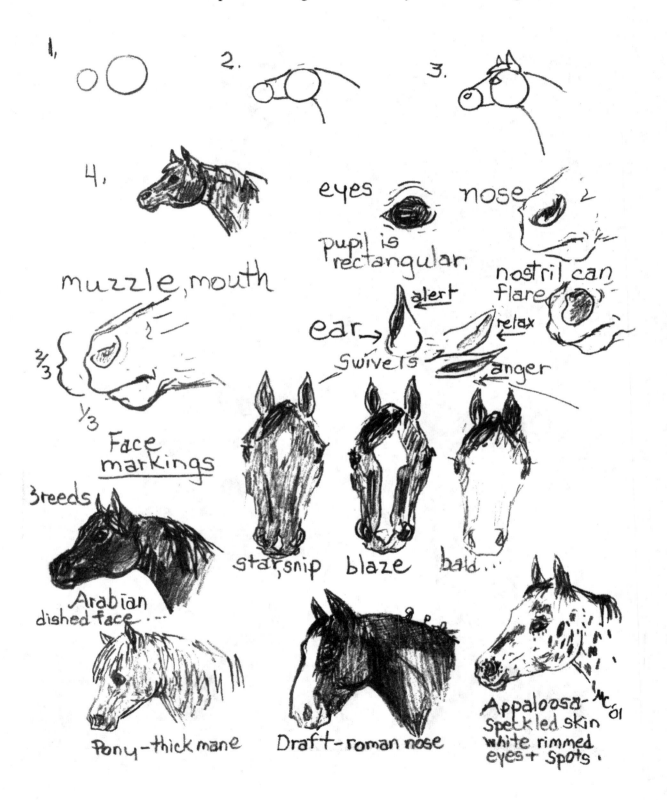

1.

2.

3.

4.

eyes

pupil is rectangular.

nose

nostril can flare

muzzle, mouth

2/3

1/3

ear → swivels

alert

relax

anger

Face markings

3reeds

star, snip

blaze

bald...

Arabian dished face...

Pony-thick mane

Draft-roman nose

Appaloosa-speckled skin white rimmed eyes + spots.

28

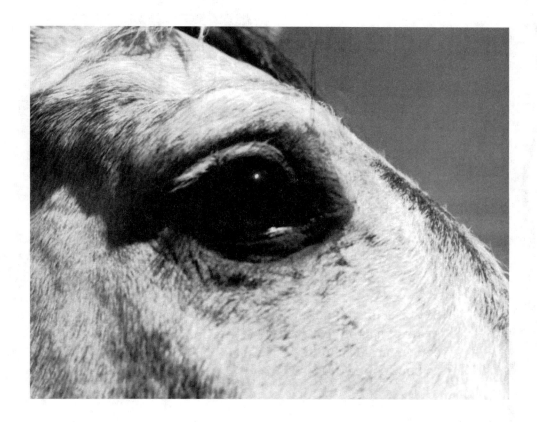

Horses have the largest eyes of any of the mammals found on land. I believe this is the most important part of the horse head in drawing. The eye is very dark with a flicker of light. You must do the eye carefully! Finish the two eyes below. Horses can see in two directions at once.

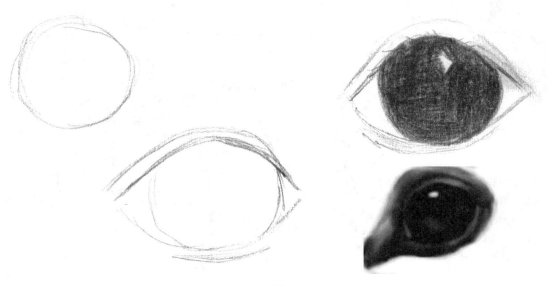

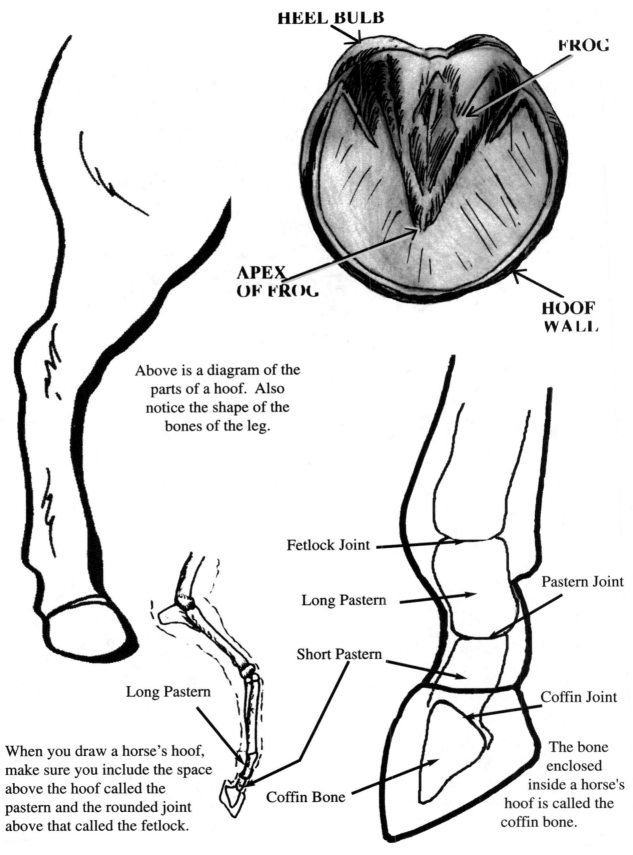

HEEL BULB

FROG

APEX OF FROG

HOOF WALL

Above is a diagram of the parts of a hoof. Also notice the shape of the bones of the leg.

Fetlock Joint

Long Pastern

Pastern Joint

Short Pastern

Coffin Joint

Long Pastern

When you draw a horse's hoof, make sure you include the space above the hoof called the pastern and the rounded joint above that called the fetlock.

Coffin Bone

The bone enclosed inside a horse's hoof is called the coffin bone.

30

Coffin bone does not point down unless there is rotation. If it points downward it could rupture the sole. That condition is usually fatal to the horse.

This is a weight bearing stance for the hoof.

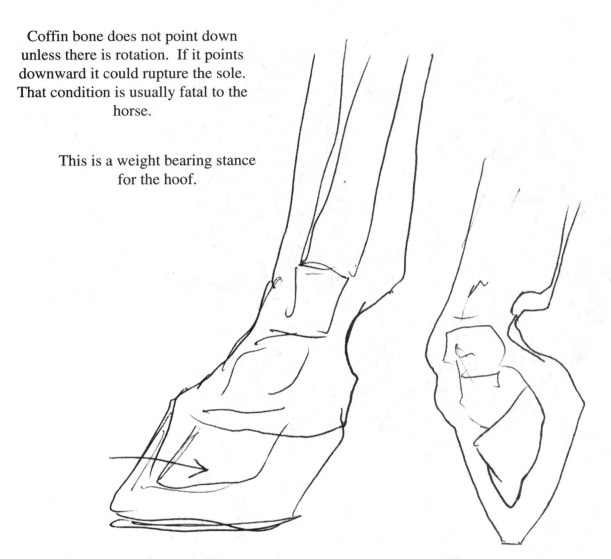

When a horse rests, sometimes he will pick his foot up and put it on its toe. Sometimes when the horse is running, his foot might also look like the one above, but it will not be on the ground.

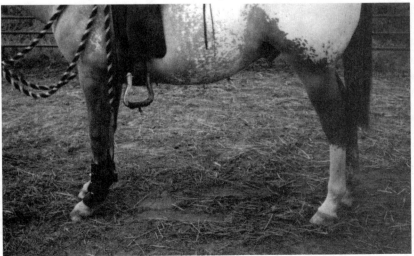

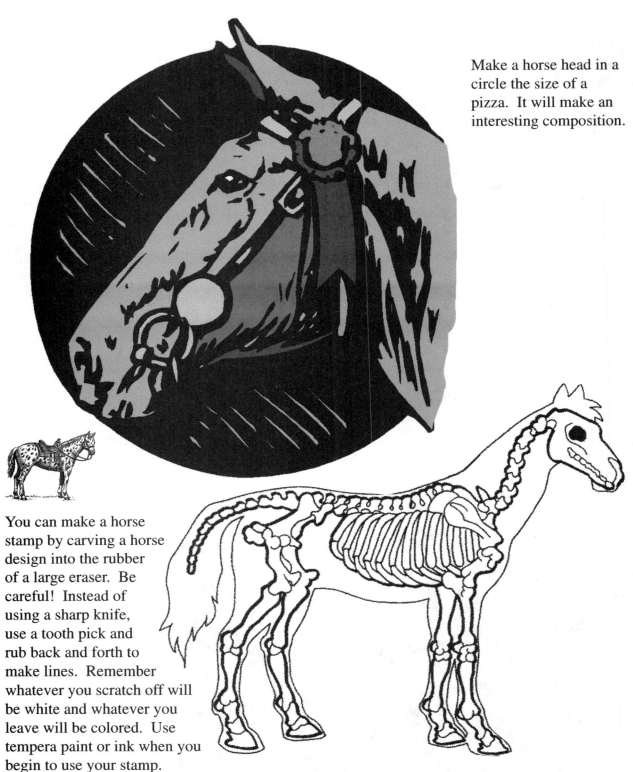

Make a horse head in a circle the size of a pizza. It will make an interesting composition.

You can make a horse stamp by carving a horse design into the rubber of a large eraser. Be careful! Instead of using a sharp knife, use a tooth pick and rub back and forth to make lines. Remember whatever you scratch off will be white and whatever you leave will be colored. Use tempera paint or ink when you begin to use your stamp.

Study closely this skeleton of a horse. Notice how the bones come together in the legs. Draw a leg of a horse just drawing the bones. This will help you to become familiar with the anatomy of a leg and learn how to draw it correctly. Start with a very lightly drawn center line, and then put the bone shapes on it.

32

Draw the other half of the horse below from the picture of the horse on the right. You may want to photocopy this page. If not, there is room to complete the picture on this page. Remember to look at the picture as a whole, don't get stuck in the details! You may want to change the background. If you put a lighter background, the horse would stand out more.

Another project idea is to cut a horse magazine picture in half and draw the other half; or cut parts out of it and draw the missing pieces.

Do a watercolor background (see watercolor lesson page 59), and then do a picture of a horse on top of the watercolor with chalk pastel. This was Audubon's technique. He discovered it quite by accident. It is told that he painted a watercolor portrait of his young bride, which turned out to be a disaster. Sometime later, he went back over the picture with chalk pastel. It was wonderful. He had discovered a mix media that worked for him.

A mix media is when you combine mediums such as: pencil and ink, watercolor and ink, cut paper and crayon etc.

Draw the other horse head seen in the picture on the left in the space above.

Do you want to draw a mother and baby horse? Notice the body size of the mother and baby. But notice that the legs are practically the same length.

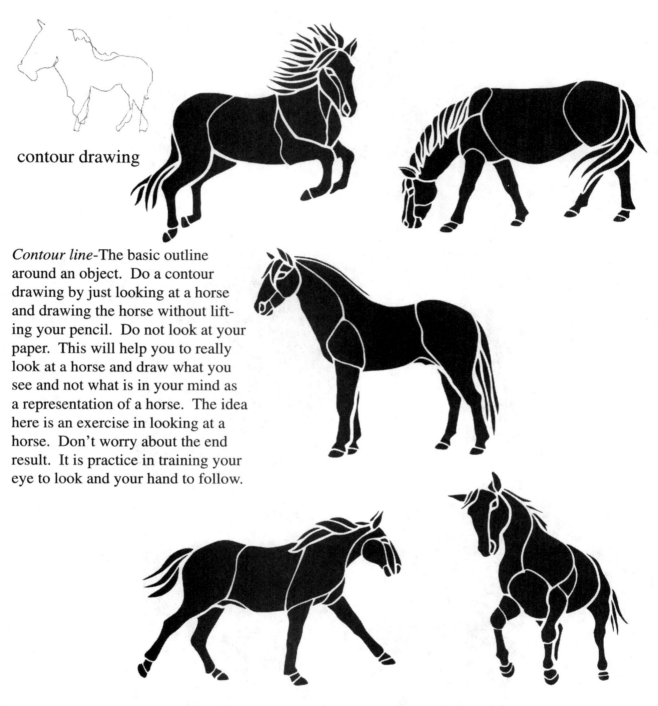

contour drawing

Contour line-The basic outline around an object. Do a contour drawing by just looking at a horse and drawing the horse without lifting your pencil. Do not look at your paper. This will help you to really look at a horse and draw what you see and not what is in your mind as a representation of a horse. The idea here is an exercise in looking at a horse. Don't worry about the end result. It is practice in training your eye to look and your hand to follow.

These horse silhouettes are a great way to practice drawing a horse. Do a contour line drawing (an outline drawing of a horse), and take a black marker and fill in different sections. Notice how diagonal lines show movement.

Use the drawing below and fill in the blank horse on the following page. Be sure to use shading. Squint your eyes to see dark and light areas and lightly color the dark areas in with your pencil. These rough lines on the following page are what you use to define basic shapes.

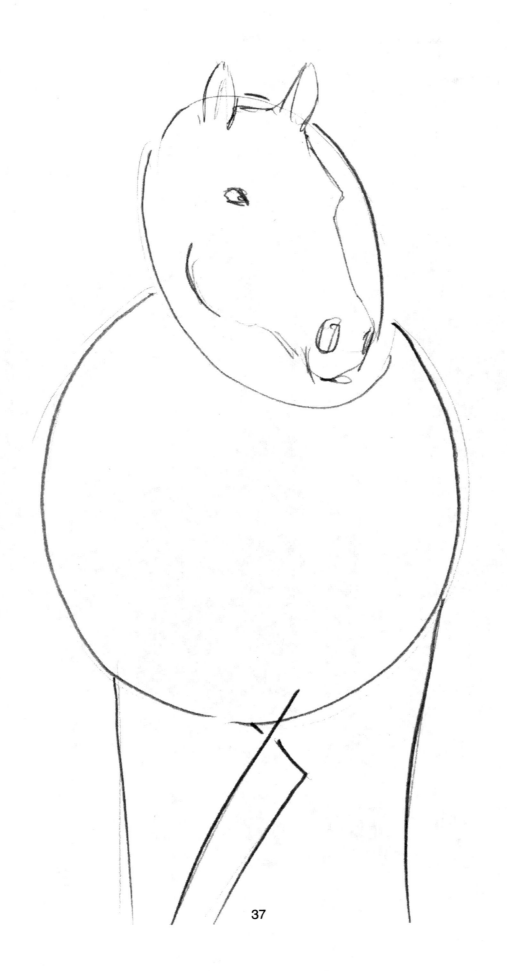

37

This drawing of a horse head was made by Richard Jeffus. It is done in pencil and called a pencil painting. Even the sky is done in pencil. On the following page is a horse head done on black paper with colored chalk.

One of our favorite projects for students is doing a horse head on black paper with colored chalk. It is a great lesson on positive/negative space. The black space is negative; the light is positive. You must have contrast to make the horse shadows look real. Review the lesson on Implied Grid on pages 16 - 20. Draw that horse on black paper using a #2 pencil. Use dark brown (burnt sienna) chalk first where you want to start shading. Don't blow the excess chalk off. It is your palette; you will need it to mix with the rest of the colors. Next, use a lighter brown (raw umber) chalk for the next lightest areas. Use yellow ochre for the lighter shades. Blend these colors together with your finger or a blending stick, smudge stick, or tortilla. Use white chalk for the star blaze on the forehead and a couple of highlights. Be careful when you remove the excess white so that it doesn't mix with the browns. You can correct any outline mistakes with black chalk, and you may want to add a little black to the darkest shadows and shaded areas. When you are pleased with the picture, spray a fine mist of fixative on it. You can buy fixative at a craft store, or you can use some hair spray. This helps keep the chalk in place.

Horses in Ancient History

On the left is a picture of horses on an Egyptian wall carving. On the right is a picture of a horse on a Grecian coin. Below are pictures of cave drawings of horses which are believed to be at least 5000 years old. Finally, on the bottom of the page you have the Roman horses ready for battle. Look at the decorations on the horses of the Romans and Egyptians. It is interesting that some of the first things artists drew were horses. Artists are still drawing horses today, so enjoy this book!

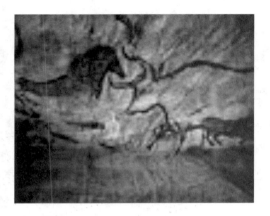

In the Middle Ages, horses were dressed very elegantly to go along with the brave knights they carried.

I will not change my horse with any that treads on four pasterns. ..He bounds from the earth, as if his entrails were hairs.....the Pegasus, ...When I bestride him, I soar, I am a hawk: he trots the air; the earth sings when he touches it; the basest horn of his hoof is more musical than the pipe of Hermes...he is pure air and fire...the Prince of Palfreys; his neigh is like the bidding of a monarch and his countenance enforces homage.
William Shakespeare   <u>Henry V</u>

In the Asian countries, horses and camels were sometimes seen side by side.

The horse is God's gift to man.   Arabian Proverb

Below is a family crest of Sir William W. Hozier. Horses were seen in heraldry designs. Design a family crest that includes a horse. Below left are a couple of designs made with a family name.

heraldry n 1: the study and classification of armorial bearings and the tracing of genealogies 2: emblems indicating the right of persons to bear arms

Viking Art

This picture is found on the upper panel of Valthjofstad Church door in Iceland. The age would be approximately the ninth through the eleventh century in the Viking age. Do these ancient warriors look like they are doing battle with dinosaurs?

Draw yourself on horseback doing battle with a dinosaur.

This is an example of a tapestry found in Oseberg, Norway. It is an example of Viking art. Notice the shape of the horses.

American Indian Art

This is a picture of a battle scene believed to be between the Blackfeet and the Sioux Indians. The feathers are supposed to indicate battles. This is a painted leather shield covering. It is from the 19th century. Native Americans would use paintings like this to record stories. Take a brown paper bag, wet it, wad it up into a ball, and then stretch it out again and let it dry. Take this leather like paper and cut out the shape of a deer skin. Using this as your story board; tell a story about your favorite horse.

VIRTUE LIBERTY U INDEPENDENCE.

The horse played a very important part in early American military history. Many gallant American soldiers on horseback carried the stars and stripes into battle.

On the following page is a picture by Edwin Forbes, the great American war correspondent for the *Frank Leslie's Illustrated Newspaper*. He did pictures of the Civil War when there was no camerman to record the history for the people back home. On the following page he pictures a war correspondent as a dashing hero. Forbes was admired for his drawings of horses. According to the book, Civil War Etchings, by William Dawson, "his horse always had the features popular in contemporary art: snorting nostrils and frantic eyes." It was in 1877 that Eadweard Muybridge took the series of magic-eye photographs that convinced everyone that horses do gallop with all four feet off the ground.

Horses on Circus Posters

Around the year 1880, there were about 35 circuses traveling America. Around 1900, there were about 75 traveling circuses. There was no television, or movie theatres, so the circus and even the Wild West Shows were popular. The horse was a main performer in these shows. There is a book titled <u>Old Time Circus Cuts</u> by Charles Philip Fox

that is filled with wonderful pictures advertising the circus coming to town. Below are just a few of the examples. I want to suggest that you make a circus or wild west poster.

Remember that a good poster has several basic criteria. The design should be bold and simple. The lettering needs to be easy to read. It needs to be as neat as possible. The design should be balanced. When younger students do a poster, they need to be sure and do the lettering in markers. A circus poster needs to convey excitement; so use some bright colors. Hot colors are red, yellow and orange.

47

Remington and Russell

Two of the greatest horse artists who ever lived are Frederic Remington and Charles Russell. They pictured the horses seen in the American west in memorable ways that the American people will cherish for centuries to come.

This picture by Remington was seen in *Harper's Weekly*, February 27, 1886. It is called "Thanksgiving at the Ranch." Did he capture what it was like for cowboys getting food on the range? Do you like this picture? Imagine if your family had to go to Grandma's house for Thanksgiving riding on horseback; what would that look like? Draw that picture!

Remington

"I knew the wild riders and the vacant land were about to vanish forever...and the more I considered the subject, the bigger the forever loomed. Without knowing how to do it, I began to record some facts around me, and the more I looked the more the panorama unfolded."

Everyone loves the American cowboys and Indians. When we are young, we pretend to be either a good cowboy, an outlaw, a lawman, an Indian, or a beautiful Indian princess. The choices are wonderful and endless. There is a famous American artist who helps us use our imagination when wondering what life in the wild west was really like. His name is Frederic Remington.

He only lived 48 years, but gave the world 2,739 pictures and 25 bronze sculptures. When he was only 16 years old he entered Yale as one of only two art students in the class. When his father died and left him a modest inheritance, he quit school and headed west in search of adventure. He probably had the same spirit of adventure to head west that so many pioneers had. After several years went by, of recording pictures of life in the west, he settled in New York and could name Teddy Roosevelt and Rudyard Kipling as companions. There is a wonderful story about Remington. The publisher Hearst sent him to Cuba to cover the Spanish American War as an artist/correspondent. Remington reportedly complained to him that there wasn't any war. Hearst cabled him the famous comment "You furnish the pictures, I'll furnish the war." Remington loved horses! His studio was built with barn doors so he could bring the horses in. He pictured every horse with its own personality....totally unique. He painted some horses galloping with all four hooves off the ground. He brought the horse to life for people who might never get to ride or see one in the old west. Teddy Roosevelt said of him, "He has portrayed a most characteristic and yet vanishing type of American life." Remington pictures are below and on the following pages. Do you think he captured the spirit of a cattle drive? He did these pictures mostly for <u>Harper's</u> <u>Weekly</u> in the late 1800's. Go to
<http://www.artcyclopedia.com/artists/remington_frederic.html>

Harper's Weekly, June 8, 1989; Frederic Remington.

49

"Geronimo and his band returning from a raid into Mexico." *Harper's Weekly*, August 18, 1888; Frederic Remington.

Ranch Life and the Hunting Trail by Theodore Roosevelt, 1888; Frederic Remington.

Here is a partial picture of a Calvary troop conducting military operations in the American dessert. They have been stopped by an Arizona sandstorm. *Harper's Weekly,* September 14, 1889; Frederic Remington.

Harper's Weekly, October 27. 1888; Frederic Remington.

Charles Russell

Charles Russell was one of the great artists who pictured the American west. He left everything and headed for Montana when he was only 16 years old. He was not only a trapper, but also lived for six months with the Blood Indians of Canada. He first started painting and drawing as a hobby, and found that his fellow westerners were happy to pay up to five silver dollars each for his pictures! According to the book, 300 Years of American Painting, by Elliot, on page 102, we have this story told by Russell himself about being asked to do a painting. "I thought I'd hit him good and hard because none of the boys had any money. Grass hadn't even started on the ranges, and our saddles were to soak, so I said fifty dollars, and I'm a common liar if the fellow didn't dig out a hundred dollars and hand them over. He thought I meant fifty dollars apiece and I got crooked as a hind's leg right away..." When he married in 1896, his wife took over the business end of his artwork. Eventually, his pictures went for as much as $10,000 each. He painted a 26 foot mural in the Montana House of Representatives about the Lewis and Clark expedition's meeting with the Flathead Indians.

Sculpting Horses

I want to share with you the differences and usability of various types of clay when sculpting horses. Horses are difficult to sculpt in a standing position without an armature. Armatures can be built of wire and wood, and then you build your clay around it. You can purchase regular **oil based modeling clay** (plasticine is a high quality of oil clay), "Rose Art," is one variety, that has many uses in art. This is good for painting (smearing) the clay on mat board or foam board, using a tooth pick, and coming up with an original two dimensional work of art. You might consider making a two dimensional sculpture of a horse. Something that stands out from the surface is two dimensional. Put the clay on cardboard or mat board and make a horse head that stands out from the surface. It is inexpensive, and for the most part, not messy. You can make a bowl shape, put a coin or medallion with a horse head standing out from the surface, press it down into the clay, and pour your Plaster of Paris into the mold, and you will have a wonderful two dimensional piece of art. We have several horse molds that we allow students to use. **Sculpey** is a wonderful clay for detail work. It can be baked into a plastic like finish and is very durable. It is not messy. It is however, expensive in relation to other clays. I always suggest purchasing this at your local discount store (WM) and saving quite a bit of money. We have found a marvelous place to purchase **terra cotta clay**. This is your natural clay that you would use to throw a pot, or build a sculpture and then fire afterwards. You can also take your clay horse to a foundry and have it bronzed. This will be very expensive! It is a very marvelous experience for children to use this type of clay. The key to this clay, is that when you purchase it, the shipping is usually as expensive as the clay. It needs to be purchased at an art store (they rarely carry it at discount stores), and is usually expensive. If you can find the outlet and go there to pick it up, you will save half of the cost. We purchase our clay at L and R Specialties in Nixa, MO. It is terrific. You will need to take the finished product and have it fired at a ceramics shop, etc. or you can choose to let it dry, paint it, and put it high on a shelf where it will not be broken. This is what we make our horse head out of with children. I made a large Indian head sculpture in high school out of terra cotta and decided not to fire it because I was afraid I had not gotten all the air bubbles out and it would explode in the kiln, (this is a chance you take). Today, it is still good and sitting in my mother's house. When it is not fired it will be fragile. **Celluclay** can be purchased at your local discount store. We have used this with large groups of students. The drawbacks are it is somewhat messy. Students need to take it home and let it dry. They need not bake it in the oven. **Play dough** is good for wee little ones, and little else, in my opinion. I have done **dough clay** projects with large groups of children in Bible school, with good success. I love the medium of **sawdust clay**. Not only is it a marvelous folk art, but the results are wonderful. We not only do it with children, but make Christmas gifts out of it for people we know. Again, we suggest making a horse head out of this variety of clay. To make your own sawdust clay just follow the recipe on the following page. Some of the most wonderful sculptures in the world of horses were made by Remington. On the following pages are three of my favorite pieces.

Over 500 years ago Leonardo da Vinci was commissioned to make a huge horse for the Duke of Milan, Italy. It was to weigh 80 tons and be 24 feet high. His full size clay model was destroyed by war and the bronze was never completed. To to these web sites for more information <http://www.leonardoshorse.org/site.asp> and <http://www.meijergardens.org/horse>.

Salt Play Clay

1/2 cup salt
1/2 cup hot water
Mix and bring to boil.
1/4 cup cold water
1/2 cup cornstarch
mix together and add mixture
to boiling liquid. Stir until stiff.
Knead when cool.

Sawdust Clay

2 cups of sawdust
3 cups of wall paper paste
Mix until you have a clay like
consistency. We suggest adding
1/4 cup of white craft glue. You
can let it air dry or bake in an
oven at 175 degrees for one
hour.

Edible Clay

1 cup smooth peanut butter
1 1/3 cups of powdered milk
3 tablespoons honey
Mix in bowl. You are ready to
sculpt and eat!

Balloon Paper Mache Horse
To make a paper mache horse you will need to mix flour and water to a soup consistency in a bowl. You will need to cut strips of paper about 2 inches thick and cover the balloons. The balloons need to shaped similar to below.

Cover seven ballons.

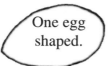

One egg shaped.

One oblong neck shape.

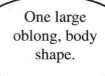

One large oblong, body shape.

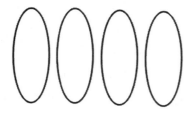

Four long or oblong ballons for the legs.

Cover each balloon with paper mache strips. Be as neat as you can. Let the baloons dry for two days.

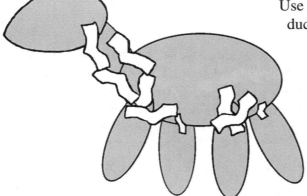

Use strong thread reinforced tape such as duct tape to tape dried mache together.

Cut pieces of mache to fit together before you tape them.

Add cardboard ears. Paper mache entire shape. Allow tow additional days to dry. Paint and add details such as eyes, whiskers and hoofs.

Bronco Buster

These are two examples of Remington's wonderful bronze sculptures.

Mountain Man

Bronco Buster

Coming Through The Rye by Remington is one of the most beautiful and majestic sculptures that Remington produced. These pictures of replicas of the sculptures were taken by Laura Noel, photographer. Thanks, Laura!

Sculpting a Horse

Start with your clay in a long potato shape. Bend it in half. It will look like a cashew nut. When sculpting, it is important to keep the object rotating in your hands. You want to be working on all sides at once. You don't want to stay working on one side. If you did, you might get finished and one side looks like a horse, and the other a hubcap! Make your clay into the basic shape

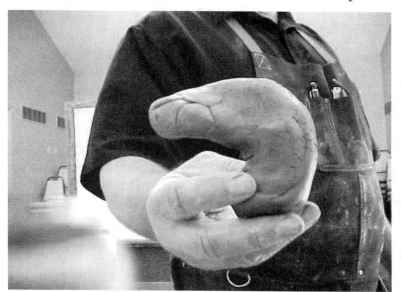

below and then set it on a flat surface so you can be sure that it will stand alone when you are finished.

What I like to do is to take the basic horse head shape and hold it in the position I want it in when it is finished. (I may want the nose up or turned downward.) Then I take it and gently slap it down on a flat surface. This forms the base of the horse's neck into a base.

Here, the nostril hole is being located. It is not directly in front, but to the side of the horse's head.

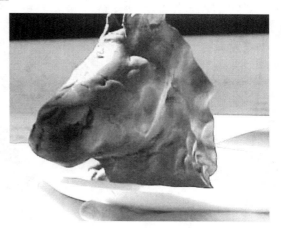

Here, I pinch the back of the horse's neck to start forming the mane. If you are using pottery clay and the clay starts cracking, just add a little water to the clay by wetting your hands. A little water goes a long way. If you use too much water, the clay will really stick to your hands.

In the picture on the left you can see the use of a pencil to create the nose and mouth. The pencil is shoved in deep and then pulled toward the side to make a crease in the skin. When doing the mouth, I draw a line across the front of the head below the nostril. I do this in order to keep the mouth straight. I continue the line past the nostril and then press it in deep and pull to the side to create the folds around the edge of the mouth.

Here I am placing the eyes. It is not a good idea to do it this way if you are going to fire it in a kiln. It is a good method to make sure the eyes are directly across from each other. Nobody wants a cockeyed horse. This is an easy way. It does, however, tend to leave air bubbles in the

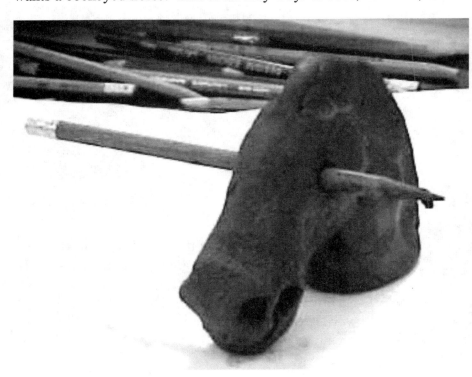

clay behind the finished eye, and if it is fired, it could explode. If you are going to air dry or are using oil based clay that you do not fire, this is a good way. Also, sculpey clay is baked not fired. It remains soft, like a chocolate cookie, until it cools from the oven. Because it is soft, any trapped air doesn't seem to bother it.

This is an example of an eye. It is made by first pushing a hole in the clay that forms an eye socket. Next, you make an eyeball that fits into the socket. I then take two separate pieces of clay shaped like a short, fat worm and place one above the eyeball and one below. I then press the clay together to eliminate any lines.

In this figure the eyeball has been placed into its socket. The two eyelids will come later.

This horse's ear is made by making a small carrot shaped piece of clay and sticking your fingernail into it to form the inside of the ear. I put the ear on the top of the head, and make sure it is well attached.

Your finished horse will look something like this one. The good thing about clay is if you don't like your finished product, just smash it and start again. Pottery clay can air dry. It can be painted with acrylic paint or coated with some kind of varnish or clear acrylic coat. Just painting it with white craft glue works wonderfully and makes a good finish. If the clay is never fired, you can make it workable again by simply putting the clay into a plastic bag and adding a little water. Your finished horse head will be quite durable. I wouldn't recommend using it for a door stop, or as a hockey puck; but if you put it on a shelf it will last for years!

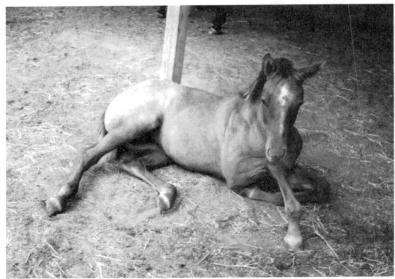

On the left is a picture of Sweet Tart. It is much easier to sculpt a horse setting down than standing up. To do a standing horse you need an armature. An armature is a framework serving as a supporting core for clay sculpture. Without an armature to support your clay, your horse will lay down anyway. To make this project simple, use Sculpey clay and do a horse laying down. Below, the finished horse sculpture was photographed and placed into the original picture of Sweet Tart.

In the picture below, you see a white ball of sculpey clay. In the next picture, you take the clay and pull out the edges. Continually move your clay in all angles in your hand. In the series of pictures below, you can see a horse gradually being shaped. The horse is shaped as though you were going to stand it up, but instead, you set the horse down. You then position his legs in the above position. You will have a sculpture of a small foal.

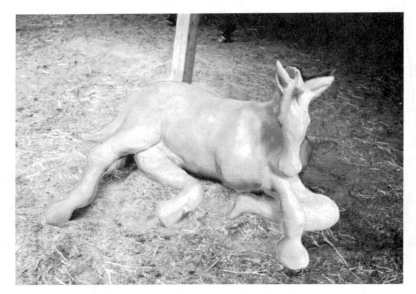

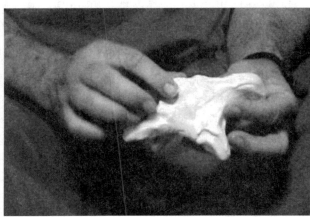

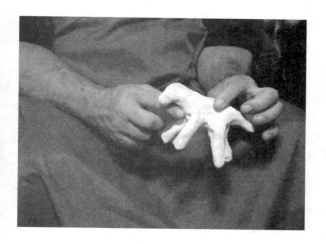 

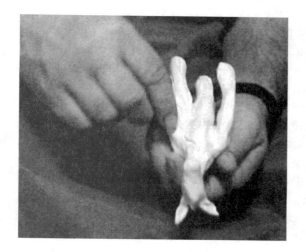 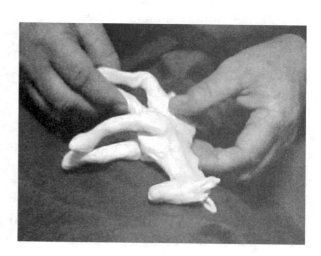

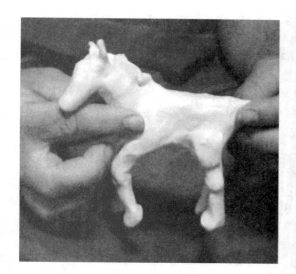 

Just like drawing a horse you start by getting a basic shape of a horse. You then continue to refine the shape adding more and more details. Sculpey clay is baked in a regular oven at 275 degrees. It is baked for 15 minutes for each 1/4 inch in thickness. A one inch thick horse will take about one hour to bake. After it is backed and cooled, it can be painted.

Watercolor

There are two different techniques to watercolor that are most often used. They are wet brush technique and dry brush technique. First, you need to be sure you are using heavy paper. You can purchase special watercolor paper at most craft stores and I recommend doing that. It will have a tooth (or texture) to it. Do not erase, (this is very important), on the surface of your paper as that will affect the color. You want your watercolor to have a transparent effect. A good watercolor artist is a master at using just the right amount of color and using the white of the paper for light. A wet brush technique would be to tape the paper to a surface so that the edges will not roll up. You then completely wet your paper (with a large brush, sponge or spray) and the colors explode into shapes and textures that you like. You can allow this to dry, and then come back and do detailing. A dry brush technique is done by just wetting one area at a time and doing the picture in sequence. Say, you do the sky first; then you do the horizon line and the tree line; and finally you wet the front of the paper for the foreground. After doing some simple watercolor pictures, let's be inventive and try some different techniques. Remember, every watercolor artist has their own way of painting.

There are some wonderful techniques you can employ to make your watercolor works have unique and interesting designs. When you sprinkle salt onto a wet color surface you can get some beautiful results. Starlike bloom shapes appear. Letting paint run and then using a low heat blow dryer to achieve a wavy effect also works well. Using a razorblade or exacto knife to scratch the surface of the paper creates an interesting effect. Putting an actual leaf or shape from nature on your paper and sponging around it also creates a nice shape. You can also use drafting tape to create a clear edge. Make sure you are using quality paper with all these techniques. Good watercolor paper is at least 80 pound paper and has a tooth. Masking tape can also be used, but it may leave a slight gummy residue. Putting torn tape on the page in interesting shapes makes land formations and cloud shapes that are very pleasing. When you gently pull the tape away, you have interesting shapes that you can leave or change. It is always important to plan the way that the viewer will see the picture. Again I say, do not erase as that will damage the surface of your paper. The artist uses shape repetition, color, areas of texture, shapes, etc. to plan the movement of the eye.

There is nothing quite like the experience of watching a watercolor master artist tackle a piece of paper. After seeing several do this, I have come to the conclusion there is no one perfect way. Practice doing both techniques several times. Sketch your horse lightly in pencil first on a piece of scrap paper. Turn your paper over and color the whole piece of paper on the back of your horse you have drawn with pencil. You are creating a piece of carbon paper with your pencil. Put your horse picture over the piece of watercolor paper and trace around the horse you have drawn on the scrap paper with your pencil. It will leave a very light outline for you to fill in. See the next page.

Step one is to transfer your drawing to a piece of watercolor paper.

I always begin by doing the eye first. I then do the chin and pull the color with water to show shading.

Remember that a watercolor picture is transparent. You need to put light colors, and add more color for shading.

Continue adding details and shading until you are satisfied.

The pictures on the right are done in watercolor. Draw your horse lightly in pencil first, and then use just a small bit of color for the body, and dark colors for the mane and tail. Study the picture carefully. Go to this web site to see a wonderful picture. <http://www.artofhorses.com/>

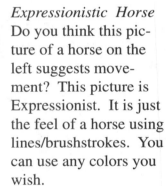

Expressionistic Horse Do you think this picture of a horse on the left suggests movement? This picture is Expressionist. It is just the feel of a horse using lines/brushstrokes. You can use any colors you wish.

The style of the horse on the left is called Sumei and originated in Japan. The style requires an artist to capture the essence of something with as few lines as possible. Making the complex simple is very difficult! Can you just use line and get the feel of a horse? First, do the project with a marker, then use a paint brush.

This horse was done for the book cover. It is a mixed media picture. It is an acrylic painting on the top and a photograph on the bottom. When you paint, you can change the picture you are painting any way you want. I could have painted this horse standing on the surface of the moon if I had wanted.

Tips on Painting on Canvas

It is a good idea to take a painting class if one is offered near where you live. A Bob Ross class gives you experience in technique and color, and although your finished picture will look exactly like everyone else, you still learn a great deal. Other art teachers offer weekly classes, and taking several from one teacher is always a good idea. The important thing about painting on canvas to remember is that you can always paint over your mistakes. When I started my first college painting class, our teacher had us do our first canvas 18" by 24" using a two inch wide brush. I had been used to working somewhat smaller, so that really taught me quite a bit. This lesson is on acrylic painting, because I never did oil painting except as a one time thing. It is a good idea to resolve not to be discouraged about what your finished painting will look like until you have done a sizable quantity of paintings. I like the fast drying quality of acrylic. One thing that is very important is to learn how to do an under painting, and then to detail. Shading can be done with subtle washes. What is a wash? That is when you add paint to water and get a light shade of the color you want to shade with. Let us say that you are painting an apple. You start with a pure red. Now you take a yellow ochre color and add lots of water to the color and you paint it over the red (after the red is dry). You can also get a dark sienna and do the same thing to one side of the apple to shade it. You can continue to do washes until you are satisfied with the results. We have talked about a variety of techniques. I love to do clouds using a sponge and occasionally I used my finger for effect. In the picture on the previous page, the background was first completed, then the horse was painted in starting from the top of the picture and going down.

This horse was painted by Michael Helm of Salem, MO.

First, choose a picture of a horse that you truly love. Do the picture in either oil pastel or chalk pastel first. This will help when you begin blending and mixing paint. The practice of drawing the horse first on a separate sheet of paper is a good way to get it just like you want before you start painting. Do a grid or an implied grid of the picture you want to paint. Once the drawing is just like you want it, transfer it to your canvas. You can either redraw the picture directly on the canvas, or you can do a pressure transfer. To make a pressure transfer, turn your drawing over. Take a soft pencil and cover the back of your picture with heavy pencil lead. Turn it back over and place it on your canvas. Go over any line you want to keep; pressing hard with a dull pencil. Keep the original picture in a safe place until the painting is finished.

Richard Jeffus copied "St. George and the Dragon" by the master artist Raphael.

After you have your picture drawn on your canvas, get your paint ready. A palette is the colors you choose for your picture. Choose the colors you want for the background first. Put your chosen colors on either a palette purchased at a craft store, or on a styrofoam plate. A couple of drops of clean water, mixed into the acrylic paint, will help it flow and mix better. Start by painting the background. Place your lighter colors on the horizon line. Don't forget to put a little

(very little) daub of yellow ocher in your white for the sky. Be careful if you get too much-- it will turn your blue sky green! Place your darkest blue on the top of your canvas. Use a broad brush and long horizontal strokes. Don't worry about covering up your horse drawing. You drew it the first time, you can draw it again. The first drawing was to see how it fits on the canvas. If you did the pressure transfer, you can

place it back on the canvas just like you did the first time. Complete the background. The more you go over the background, the more it will blend together. If the paint gets a little sticky or doesn't seem to be blending well, add a little water. The best way to add water is with your brush. If you want to darken the horizon, start with a clean brush at the top and use an overlapping horizontal stroke; go back and forth working your way toward the horizon. If you want the top of the sky lighter, start with a clean brush on the horizon line and work toward the top. You can adjust the ground line in the same manner. Once you have the general colors you want for your sky and ground, start working on the details. In the picture on the left you can see the mountains, trees and a fence all were added before the horse was even started. The bottom picture has been finished. Notice, how the horse seems to leap out of the background. There isn't any edge of white unpainted canvas around the horse. You can also see that the background is continuous around the horse. Some people try to paint the horse first and then try to paint the background around it. When you do it that way, it is always hard to match the background around the horse. Notice how the shadow helps the picture look more realistic.

This picture by Richard Jeffus is a statement on evolution. Whenever someone says, "Show me something that has evolved," this is the thing sited most often. It is called the "Horse Series." The evolutionists claim that this series proves that animals evolved. They say that the "Dawn Horse," *Eohippus,* turned into an *Orohippus* which continued to evolve until it became a horse. There are many problems with this series. It is based on the fact that all of these animals have three toes. They also believe that this same animal turned into a rhinoceros and an elephant. All of this because they all have three toes. You could say most cars have four wheels so they are all related. How about, everything that is square is related, from sugar cubes to cardboard boxes, to buildings, are all related because they are all square? Having similar features does not indicate a common ancestor. They may indicate a common designer, or overcoming a common problem. All bridges have a lot of similarities because they all do one thing in common. They span from one side of an obstacle to the other. Three toes in common doesn't prove horses are related. It has been proven through DNA testing that the supposed connections never happened. Most reputable scientists know there isn't any connection. It is still taught as proof of evolution because there are so few cases where supposed transitions have taken place. If you look for transitions between a spoon and a fork, and you look long enough, you can find enough forms between them to prove that one evolved from the other. It does not prove anything. This only proves that all spoons and forks have a common creator, and he is creative, and the things he creates have a purpose. They are designed to eat with. The horse, rhinoceros, and man all have a created purpose...to serve God. This is what I am saying in this picture.

Horses pull sleighs, carriages, and Conestoga wagons.

Complementary colors are colors opposite each other on the color wheel (see below). There are only three sets of complementary colors. Each set consists of a primary and a secondary color. Most students want to know why it is important to know something. Artists always do one thing. They take three dimensional things like horses, cats and flowers and make one dimensional art out of them. They do this by: shading, shadows and textures. Most people think that you shade a color with black to make it darker. Most artists, however, say, "Never, never, never use black. Black is death to a picture." If you need to darken an object you can use the color opposite on the color wheel. To shade a red apple, use green. To shade a yellow banana, use purple. To shade an orange pumpkin, use blue. One small problem is when you try to shade a purple grape, you cannot make purple darker by putting yellow in it. In the case of purple and blue you use the complementary color to highlight it. The picture above of the horse on a hill was done entirely in yellow with purple shading. The picture doesn't look natural, but has an expressionistic look to it. The project for this lesson is to do a picture entirely with complementary colors. The finished picture will not look natural. That is okay. The purpose of this lesson is to get you away from using black to shade. Do a horse drawing only using complementary colors.

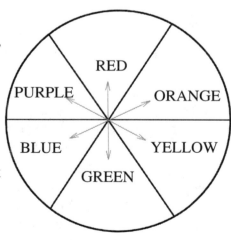

For a free coloring book of different kinds of horses go to <http://awhitehorse.com/horses/>.

Here are some horse pictures you can use for inspiration.

The wagon rests in winter, the sleigh in summer, the horse never.
Yiddish Proverb

Folk Art Horses From Different Cultures

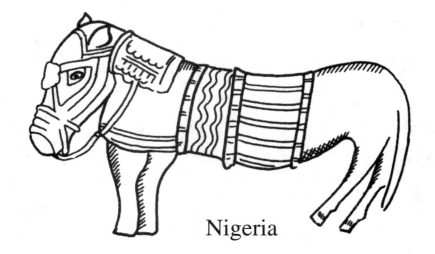

Nigeria

Study these horses carefully. Do you notice the shading on the horses? Can you make a horse outline with patterns and interesting designs that is just symbolic of the horse?

Sweden

A good man will take care of his horses and dogs, not only while they are young, but also when they are old and past service.
Plutarch

The Swedish Dala horse carries a rich history dating back to the 18th century. These colorful horses are painted with the richly colored flower patterns like those of the Dala paintings used to decorate furnishings and walls.

Panama Horse

American Folk Art Horse

Greece

Russia

Folk Art
This is art originating among the common people of a nation or region and usually reflecting their traditional culture, especially everyday or festive items produced or decorated by unschooled artists. Horses have always played an important part in folk art.

Horse Cookies

Do you love horses enough that you would like to make cookies in the shape of a horse? In the book Authentic Pennsylvania Dutch Designs by Frances Lichten, these designs of horse cookie cutters are found. Here is a recipe for cookies you can use. Roll out your dough and draw a horse shape on the dough. Use a butter knife to cut out your design.

Easy Sugar Cut-Outs

2 C. flour
1/2 tsp. baking powder
1/2 tsp. salt
3/4 C. butter
3/4 C. sugar
1 large egg
1 tsp. vanilla

In bowl combine flour, baking powder and salt. In another bowl, beat butter and sugar until light and fluffy. Beat in egg, and vanilla. Stir in the flour mixture until just combined. Divide dough into quarters. Wrap and refrigerate 4 hours. Preheat oven to 350 degrees. Grease cookie sheets. Roll one dough quarter 1/4 - 1/8 " thick between 2 sheets of wax paper.

There is something about the outside of a horse that is good for the inside of a man.
Sir Winston Churchill

74

There are only three kinds of horses that are truly considered wild horses. These are the zebras, the wild asses, and the Mongolian horses. All other horses and donkeys are called domestic horses. Domestic horses that have escaped into the wild are called *feral* horses.

These are wild horses from the southwestern United States called feral horses.

This is an Indian sitting on a pinto (spotted) pony. The background is a western landscape. Here is a great idea for a project. Tear this page out of your horse book, or copy the page on a copy machine. Color the back of the picture completely putting pressure on your black crayon. This will act like carbon paper. Put the finished picture on a piece of brown wrapping paper or brown paper bag and trace the picture with your pencil. It will leave lines on the brown and then you can color your picture with oil or chalk pastels, or crayons.

A Logo

Here are two horse logos. A business will hire you to design a symbol. The Nike symbol signifies a sports company. Can you design a logo for a ranch in the west?

Logo-A name, symbol or trademark designed for easy and definite recognition.

In art, *hot colors* are red, orange and yellow. Can you make a sunset using chalk pastels from these colors? Wet your paper with a rag or sponge before you begin. Be sure and use 60 pound paper (the thicker the better). You can even use brown wrapping paper. Notice how the sky is colored darker at the top and lighter as you go to the horizon line. When you are finished with your sunset, use black chalk or charcoal and draw a horse and rider similar to this picture.

Rocking Horses

Here is a baby's first horse, the "Rocking Horse." In the same way that the Teddy Bear was developed from the bear, a favorite toy was developed from looking at a horse. Can you design a "Rocking Horse" for a princess or a prince?

Horses and the Bible

Proverbs 21:31
"The horse is prepared against the day of battle: but safety is of the LORD."

Job 39:19-25 "Hast thou given the horse strength? Hast thou clothed his neck with thunder? Canst thou make him afraid as a grasshopper? The glory of his nostrils is terrible. He paweth in the valley, and rejoiceth in his strength: he goeth on to meet the armed men."

Revelation 19:11
"And I saw heaven opened, and behold a white horse; and he that sat upon him was called Faithful and True, and in righteousness he doth judge and make war."

The following two pictures are by Gustave Dore. They appear in his *Family Illustrated Bible*. He worked primarily in the mid 1800's. He illustrated *Don Quixote*, *Paradise Lost* and *Divine Comedy* to name just a few. These are wood block prints. An easy way to experience printing at home is to save a foam meat tray. Be sure it is cleaned and washed before you begin. Draw a horse using your pencil being sure to indent the lines into the tray. Now you can paint the tray completely and then print at least 3 times. You can enhance the design with markers or colored pencils. You can even develop your own line of greeting cards!

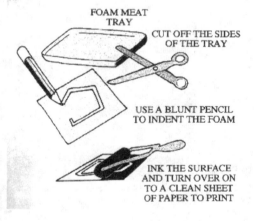

FOAM MEAT TRAY

CUT OFF THE SIDES OF THE TRAY

USE A BLUNT PENCIL TO INDENT THE FOAM

INK THE SURFACE AND TURN OVER ON TO A CLEAN SHEET OF PAPER TO PRINT

This is a picture of the good Samaritan from Luke 10:33, 34.

Zechariah 6:5

This picture is the vision of the four chariots in Zechariah 6:5.

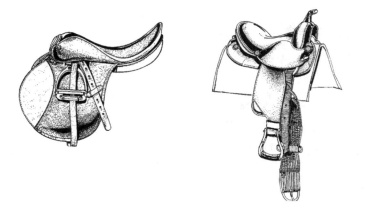

Saddles

On the left is an English saddle and on the right is a western saddle. It is important to study these designs so your saddle on your horse will look authentic.

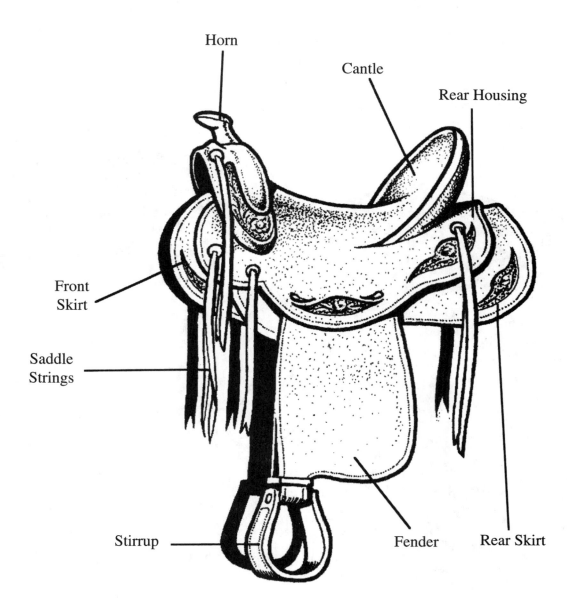

Horn

Cantle

Rear Housing

Front Skirt

Saddle Strings

Stirrup

Fender

Rear Skirt

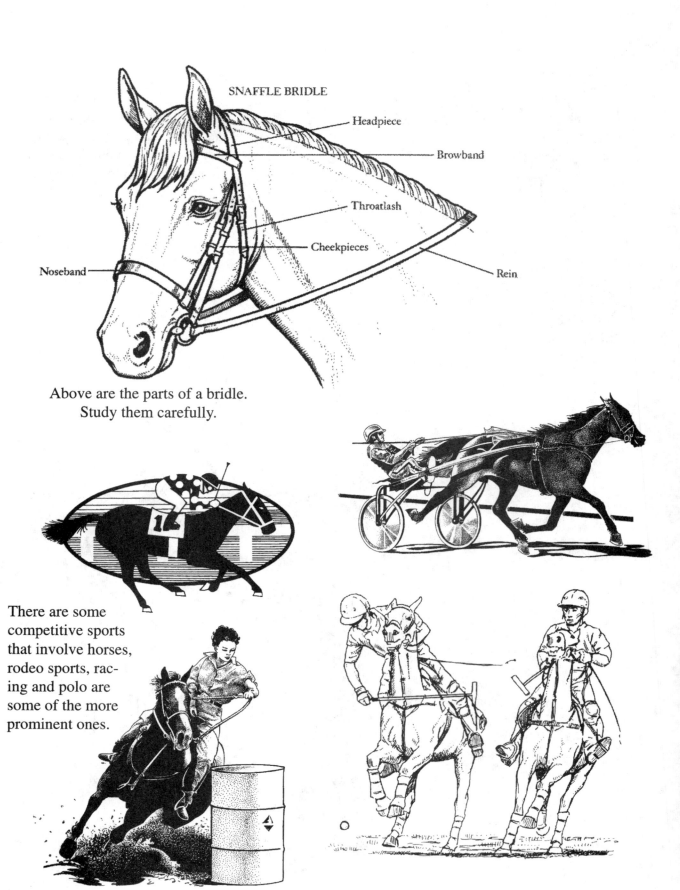

SNAFFLE BRIDLE

Headpiece

Browband

Throatlash

Cheekpieces

Noseband

Rein

Above are the parts of a bridle.
Study them carefully.

There are some competitive sports that involve horses, rodeo sports, racing and polo are some of the more prominent ones.

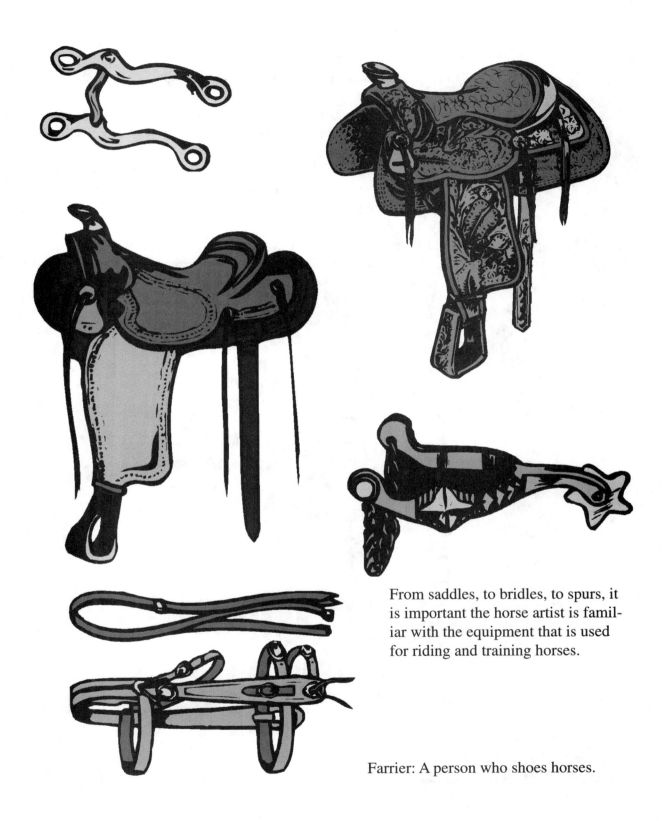

From saddles, to bridles, to spurs, it is important the horse artist is familiar with the equipment that is used for riding and training horses.

Farrier: A person who shoes horses.

Comic Strip Horses

Now is the time to make your own comic character horse. There are 3 things to remember when you are drawing a comic strip or creating a comic character.

1. A cartoon is an exaggeration. Make sure you do this when you make up your comic horse. Notice the parts of the horses below that are too big or too small.

2. A cartoon is a stereotype. If you are doing a cowboy horse, dress him as a cowboy. If you are doing a horse that is from the time of knights and dragons, dress him to go with it. A race horse will look very differently from a plow horse.

3. A cartoon captures the essence of things in as few lines as possible. Props are used to help create a story or scene. These can be drawn with an outline to just suggest their presence.

Make your own comic strip that is funny.

Design a book cover, a CD cover, or a video tape cover with a horse on it.

My good friend Joni Johnson is a western artist. She loves horses so much, look above to see how she signs her name. She always draws a horse and a cross when she signs her name. She is a wonderful art teacher and can be contacted at Rt.1 Box 163, Wayne, OK 73095 or call 405-449-3557.

My husband calls this picture his "horsefly."

86

Do a horse or western landscape in a *monochromatic* color scheme. Use only the color blue and black or white. Then do a white horse (bottom) or a black horse in the snow. Be sure and use your practice drawings from the previous pages when drawing your horse.

Believe it or not, these beautiful horses are Chinese cut paper designs. Chinese cut paper designs were found as early as the Tang dynasty (618-906 A.D.). It is well known in recent times as a popular folk art. Scissors can be used, however, sometimes professional paper cutters use exacto knives or gouges to get fine details. Use black or brown paper and make a similar design to these horses. You could even enlarge one of these on a copy machine. Once you have your pattern, you can make many. Glue your finished horse on brightly colored paper. You can draw your own horse shape. You can cut out as many white areas as you want. Have fun!

Do a six hour drawing of a horse. Work on this over several days so you will be able to do one with lots of details and complexity. Draw until you loose your concentration. When you feel rested, start where you left off. Remember to use shading, shadow and texture. The reason for the time frame is so that you will do a drawing with lots of details.

Diagonal lines in art always show movement. Notice that because the horse is in a diagonal position, it looks like movement is taking place. Remington drew a horse with all four feet off the ground in a running position. At that time in history, people didn't believe that this position was possible. Time proved him right!

Pegasus

Below is a fantasy picture of a winged horse. A winged horse is called a Pegasus. Pegasus was a winged horse, which according to mythology sprang from the body of Medusa at her death. Can you imagine a horse with fins and gills? Draw an imaginary horse combining elements of other animals.

A seahorse is an animal who rides the prairies of the sea!

The World's Largest Horse

It is a purebred Belgian stallion by the name of Brooklyn Supreme. He stood 19.2 hands (6'6")
at his withers. He weighed over 3,200 pounds and is entered in the Guiness Book of World
Records. He was foaled in 1928 and died in 1948. This photo was taken when he was fully
mature. He lived in Iowa.

Read the following description
below of General Robert E.
Lee's horse Traveler. Can you
write a description of your
favorite horse?

The following is written by General Robert E. Lee to Markie Williams who wished to paint a
portrait of Lee's horse, "Traveller"

*If I was an artist like you, I would draw a true picture of Traveller; representing his fine propor-
tions, muscular figure, deep chest, short back, strong haunches, flat legs, small head, broad forehead, delicate ears, quick eye, small feet, and black mane and tail. Such a picture would inspire
a poet, whose genius could then depict his worth, and describe his endurance of toil, hunger,
thirst, heat and cold; and the dangers and suffering through which he has passed. He could
dilate upon his sagacity and affections, and his invariable response to every wish of his rider. He
might even imagine his thoughts through the long night marches and the days of battle through
which he has passed. I am no artist Markie, and can therefore only say he is a Confederate grey.*

Tails   the "living" End

flowing

foal fuzzy

"high tailin it"

docked

some Hackneys
some draft,

arched
or set tail.
5 gaited-
full

3 gaited
shaved

hunter braid-

MC

The Horse's Tail

Our dear friend and horse artist Martha Cunningham wanted to share some information on the "glorious tail," as she calls it. An ancient tale says a fleeing nomad cast off his cloak to find that his noble Arabian horse with naturally arched tail carriage had caught and carried his cloak! Tails denote disposition, action, breed, geographic and periodic styles and more. The American Saddle and Tennessee Walker breeds use "set tails." The Western Cowhorses of the 1850's and 1860's had tails trimmed near their hocks (the joint bending backwards in the hind leg of a horse). Manes were roached (to cut a mane to stand up), to avoid entanglements with lariats. Short fuzzy tails are the indicator of a foal or baby horse.

Equus

Cantherius   *Wallach*

Here are some beautiful examples of horse tails and manes. Look at the shaded areas on the tail. Can you make a tail or mane look like this?

Practice drawing tails of horses below.

Cirrus clouds are called mare's tails. A cirrus cloud is defined as the type of white cloud that resembles a wispy filament. What can you compare to a horse's tail?

The End

Visual Manna offers art workshops all over the country. We do workshops on drawing, painting, and sculpting horses, and all areas of art training. We offer specialized camps for the arts. Visual Manna also offers wonderful workshops in other arts such as drama, music/musical theatre and photography and cinema. Contact us for more information at: 1-573-729-2100 or email us at: arthis@rollanet.org. Visit our website at: <http://www.visualmanna.com>

Sharon Jeffus has a B.S.S.E. in art education from John Brown University and ten years experience teaching in the public schools. She began homeschooling her children in 1991. Since 1993, Visual Manna has been in business and Sharon and Richard have been teaching art to support groups across America. Sharon has written various curriculum and programs, including one for the Cherokee Indians that was rated outstanding by the Bureau of Indian Affairs. Sharon has written a complete art curriculum that reinforces the core curriculum subjects. She also is certified to teach ESL (English as a Second Language) and has taught Intensive English at the University of Missouri at Rolla and written Teaching English Through Art. Sharon studied sculpting at Southern Illinois University and painting at Metropolitan in Denver. Richard Jeffus is a licensed counselor, licensed minister and family therapist who spent nine years counseling at a Missouri treatment center. He is also a graduate of John Brown University. He resigned to be CEO of Visual Manna and to do his Christian art work. He makes life sized dinosaurs and does beautiful, award winning Christian art. He has illustrated all of Visual Manna's books and is presently illustrating several books for others. Being a professional illustrator and sculptor, he shares techniques with students.

Our Philosophy of Teaching Art

Thank you for your inquiry into our programs. Our philosophy of teaching art is: First and foremost, God is a creative God and we were created in His image. This means that we possess some of the attributes of God, only in a finite way. We believe each child is imbued by God to be innately creative. It is our goal to bring out that special and precious creativity and individuality in each child that we teach. We believe it is important to introduce them to many different mediums and various techniques so that they can have the skills needed to express their creativity. We believe the study of the master works of art can facilitate the student's understanding of how techniques have been applied in the past. This gives understanding of how previous masters have overcome various technical problems to express their creativity more fully.

Most education today is geared to rote memorization and regurgitation of the facts, techniques and methods. Many times art is taught in a similar method to math, science, history or English. Pressure to perform to arbitrary standards is often placed on students restricting their creativity to the demands of conformity and to the need for expedience in measuring performance in relationship to the norm. Creativity is as individual and unique as snowflakes. If three architects are presented with a design problem for a particular building, they will all solve the problem differently. Art students should be taught and encouraged to study a variety of techniques and methods. They can then discover solutions to their design problems, and come up with their own unique creation.

So many of the greatest minds in history were independent problem solvers and thinkers. That is our goal for each Visual Manna student. In the teaching of techniques, vocabulary and art appreciation, we strive to produce students that have a well rounded and thorough understanding of art, using their creativity and individuality to the maximum. We have art camps and study for advanced students available taught from a Christian perspective.

Visual Manna Product List

Did you enjoy this book? Here are some more wonderful selections from Visual Manna.

Master Drawing $14.95
ABC's of Art $10.95
Visual Manna Complete Art Curriculum $68.00
Visual Manna's Teaching History Through Art $19,95
Visual Manna's Teaching English Through Art $17.95
Visual Manna's Teaching Geography Through Art $19.95
Visual Manna's Teaching Science Through Art $14.95
Visual Manna's Preschool/Early Elementary Art and Art Appreciation $14.95
Visual Manna's Teaching American History through Art $14.95
Visual Manna's Dinosaur Art Project Book $10.95
Visual Manna's Younger Student Art Kit $39.95
Visual Manna's Older Student Art Kit $39.95
Visual Manna's Complete Color Art Kit $89.95
Visual Manna's Master Drawing Video Kit $49.95
Visit our web site at <http://www.visualmanna.com> or call us at 1-888-2757309 and order Visa/Mastercard today. Send for your free catalog and project newsletter.
Visual Manna, P.O. Box 553, Salem, MO 65560. All orders pay 15%PH.